Destinati

BURY PUBl

This book must be returr
recorded below to the Library from which it was borrowed.

19. JUL 1991 22 AUG 1991 -9 SEP 1991 12. OCT 1991 -8 NOV 1991 -3 MAR 1992 12 MAR 1992 27 APR 1992 *Paid*	*Par*	

AUTHOR	CLASS No.
MIDDLETON J.	448.3
TITLE Destination France	BOOK No.
	3/91

H

RAMSBOTTOM

Acknowledgements

With thanks to Christopher, Robert, Duncan, Adam and Sharon, from Cedars Upper School, Linslade, whose experiences inspired this book and who contributed their suggestions to it.

The authors and publishers would like to thank the following for supplying photographs:
Stuart Boreham: pp. 10, 21, 32, 34, 37, 38, 47, 56 (bottom left)
Keith Gibson: pp. 30, 45, 48
Roddy Paine: pp. 15, 22, 26, 39, 41, 43, 56 (top right)
Zefa Picture Library (UK) Ltd: p. 35

British Library Cataloguing in Publication Data
Middleton, Josephine
  Destination France: a handbook for school visits.
  1. France – Visitors' guides
  I. Title II. Smith, Mary
  914.4'04838

ISBN 0 340 52805 2

First published 1990

© 1990 J. Middleton and M. Smith   Illustration © Katinka Kew
Cover illustration © Sue Dray

All rights reserved. No part of this publication may be reproduced or transmitted in any form or by any means, electronic or mechanical, including photocopy, recording, or any information storage and retrieval system, without permission in writing from the publisher or under licence from the Copyright Licensing Agency Limited. Further details of such licences (for reprographic reproduction) may be obtained from the Copyright Licensing Agency Limited, of 33–34 Alfred Place, London WC1E 7DP.

Typeset by Wearside Tradespools, Fulwell, Sunderland
Printed in Hong Kong for the educational publishing division of Hodder and Stoughton Ltd, Mill Road, Dunton Green, Sevenoaks, Kent by Wing King Tong

Contents

Introduction — the aims of this book; explanation of symbols; how to use the book — 5

Don't Worry — what to say when you don't understand or people speak too quickly; use of *vous* and *tu*; reminders of polite usage of *Monsieur/Madame*, *s'il vous plaît* and *merci* — 6

Meeting the Family — exchanging greetings; answering questions about the journey and your state of health; giving a gift — 9

Settling In — finding your way around the house; how things work; your room; what to ask if you have forgotten anything you need; bed-time — 13

Fitting In — asking when it is convenient to bath/shower, telephone home; asking what time to get up, have breakfast, be ready to go out; asking permission; arrangements for washing and ironing — 17

Meals — meals and meal-time customs; accepting and declining food; offering to help; conversation at table — 21

Daily Life — things to talk about; things to do; going to school; going visiting; sporting activities; entertainment — 26

Contents

Out and About	shops you might need; shopping for postcards; opening and closing times; buying a snack; buying souvenirs, clothes; looking after money; changing money; using a public telephone; travelling alone; outings	31
Looking after your Health	a first-aid kit; self-help measures; what to do in case of illness or minor accident; going to the doctor	40
Minor Mishaps	accidental breakages; mending clothes; losing belongings; getting lost; saying no; homesickness; what to do if you don't fit in with the family	46
The End of your Stay	preparing for the trip home; thanking the family; writing a thank you letter; writing to your partner	53
Appendix	checklist of essentials to pack; comments and exclamations for a variety of situations; days, dates and times; sizes; games to play on the road	57

Introduction

There are many phrase books available for adults but these do not contain the particular information which would be helpful for a young traveller alone abroad, possibly for the first time. If you are a young person and you are going to stay with a French family, whether on a brief exchange or for a longer period of time, this is the book for you! It covers not only the French phrases which you will find useful, but also contains hints on coping with the French way of life which should help you to feel at ease in your new surroundings. Before you leave for France, read it through for general information and to practise a few phrases.

One of the aims of the visit is to improve your spoken French! Try out some of the phrases in this book in the knowledge that you are going to be understood. Even if you are not very confident, remember that it is better to attempt to say something than to say nothing.

It is easy to learn to ask the way in a foreign language; it is not always so easy to understand the answer! To help overcome this kind of problem, phrases which you might hear in a given situation are included: for example, questions which you might be asked; instructions; comments, and other information which you might be given.

Since the same idea can often be expressed in different ways, sentences of varying degrees of difficulty have been suggested where this is appropriate. These are coded as follows:

- simple sentences that even beginners can attempt;
- ▶ slightly more complex sentences;
- ■ more elegant phrasing – designed to impress!

Where there is a choice of masculine or feminine forms, examples are given in the masculine. It is advisable to start with the simplest phrase and progress to the others as your confidence increases.

If you have the cassette which accompanies this book, listen to it with the book in front of you so that you can relate the sound to the written phrase. Later, you will be able to listen to the cassette without the written French and English.

This book is pocket-sized. Take it with you wherever you go. Let it help you enjoy your stay in France.

Don't Worry

At first it may seem that French people speak very quickly, but you will get used to hearing the language at this speed and will begin to recognize words and phrases that you know. You will gradually understand the drift of what is being said, even if you can't follow every detail.

If you find it difficult to understand, these requests will help:

To your French friend

- Pardon, parle lentement, s'il te plaît. *Sorry, please speak slowly.*
- Excuse-moi, je ne comprends pas. Parle plus lentement, s'il te plaît. *I'm sorry, I don't understand. Please speak more slowly.*
- Excuse-moi, tu parles trop vite et je ne comprends pas. Veux-tu parler plus lentement s'il te plaît? *I'm sorry, you are talking too fast and I can't understand. Will you please speak more slowly?*

You may not want the sentence repeated more slowly, but phrased in more simple words.

Excuse-moi, je ne comprends pas. Veux-tu le dire plus simplement, s'il te plaît? *I'm sorry, I don't understand. Could you say it in a simpler way, please?*

Don't Worry

To adults

These phrases have the same meanings as the previous section, but are shown separately to help you adapt to using 'vous':

- Pardon, parlez plus lentement, s'il vous plaît, monsieur/madame.
- Excusez-moi, je ne comprends pas. Parlez plus lentement, s'il vous plaît, monsieur/madame.
- Excusez-moi, vous parlez trop vite et je ne comprends pas. Pouvez-vous parler plus lentement, s'il vous plaît, monsieur/madame?

'Tu' and 'Vous'

Your French friend and his/her parents will almost certainly use 'tu' when talking to you. At first it may be difficult to remember that you should use 'vous' when talking to adults but 'tu' to friends of your own age. Usually French people would think it rude if a stranger called them 'tu', but they will, of course, understand your difficulty, so if you realise you have made a mistake, just say "Pardon". They will probably help you if you get in a muddle again, and may even invite you to use 'tu' when talking to them individually. Remember that you will need to use 'vous' if you are talking to more than one person.

Don't Worry

Good Manners

> The French use more polite forms of speech than we do. When you speak to the French mother you should call her "Madame", and the French father "Monsieur"; these should also be used when talking to any other adults. It may seem very formal to you to keep saying, for example, "Oui, Monsieur," or "Non, Monsieur," – but it is perfectly normal and will be expected. When you listen to French people speaking, you will notice how common it is. You will also notice how frequently they use "S'il vous plaît" and "Merci". In this book, these are sometimes omitted, but only to avoid unnecessary repetition – don't forget that you will need to use them to be polite.

Have a go!

Remember that French people will understand your initial shyness at talking in a foreign language and they will be encouraging you all they can. Keep your sentences short at first and try to use phrases you know to be correct, either because you have used them at school or because you have seen them in these pages. As your confidence and ability grow, you may feel able to tackle longer sentences.

Bonne Chance!   *Good Luck!*

Meeting the Family

You are likely to feel tired after the long journey to reach your host family. If you learn a few phrases before you go, you will not panic when you first have to cope with French on your own. You could practise them with your friends during the journey from England.

Greetings

> When you arrive, your host family will probably shake you by the hand – but do not be taken aback if they kiss you on both cheeks or hug you; accept their greeting in the spirit it is offered! If the parents make a little speech of welcome, don't be worried if you cannot follow everything; all you need to do is to say thank you and smile.

Here are some of the things you may hear, and some possible replies:

Bonjour, ..., ça va? *Hello, ..., how are you?*

Bienvenu! *Welcome!*

Meeting the Family

Nous sommes enchantés de te recevoir chez nous. *We are very pleased to have you here.*

Nous espérons que tu vas passer un bon séjour. *We hope you will have a lovely stay.*

Bonjour, Monsieur/Madame, ça va bien, merci. *Hello, very well, thank you.*

Enchanté Monsieur/Madame. *Pleased to meet you.*

Salut! *Hello* (to friends of your age).

How was your journey?

Here are some questions you may be asked, together with some suitable answers:

Tu as fait un bon voyage? *Did you have a good journey?*
   Oui, j'ai fait un bon voyage, merci. *Yes, I had a good journey, thanks.*
   Non, je n'ai pas fait un bon voyage. *No, I didn't have a good journey.*

Le voyage s'est bien passé? *Did you have a good journey?*
   Oui, très bien, merci. *Yes, very good, thank you.*
   Pas mal, merci. *Not too bad, thank you.*

C'était une bonne traversée? *Was it a good crossing?*
   Oui, très bien, merci. *Yes, very good, thank you.*
   Non, c'était mauvais. *No, it was bad.*

Meeting the Family

Tu as eu le mal de mer? *Were you seasick?*
  Oui, j'ai eu le mal de mer. *Yes, I was seasick.*
  Je vais bien maintenant, merci. *I'm fine now, thank you.*
  Non, je n'ai pas eu le mal de mer. *No, I was not seasick.*

How do you feel?

You will probably feel rather tired after a long journey and all the new experiences. Your hosts will understand this and are almost certain to enquire about how you feel.

Tu es fatigué? *Are you tired?*
- Oui, je suis fatigué. *Yes, I'm tired.*
- Oui, je suis un peu fatigué. *Yes, I'm a bit tired.*
- Oui, je suis très fatigué. *Yes, I'm very tired.*
- Non, je ne suis pas fatigué. *No, I'm not tired.*
- Non, je ne suis pas trop fatigué. *No, I'm not too tired.*
- Non, je ne suis pas du tout fatigué. *No, I'm not a bit tired.*

  Tu veux te reposer? *Would you like to rest?*
- Oui, s'il vous plaît. *Yes, please.*
- Oui, je veux bien. *Yes, I'd like that.*
- Oui, je veux bien me reposer. *Yes, I'd like to rest.*

You may be offered something to eat and drink on your arrival.

Tu as faim? *Are you hungry?*
  Oui, j'ai faim. *Yes, I'm hungry.*
  Non, je n'ai pas faim. *No, I'm not hungry.*

Tu as soif? *Are you thirsty?*
  Oui, j'ai soif. *Yes, I'm thirsty.*
  Non, je n'ai pas soif. *No, I'm not thirsty.*

If you are very tired, you may want to refuse a meal without upsetting anybody.

- Excusez-moi, je suis fatigué. Je ne veux pas manger. *I'm sorry, I'm tired. I don't want to eat.*
- Excusez-moi, mais je suis trop fatigué pour manger. *I'm sorry, but I am too tired to eat.*
- Excusez-moi, je ne veux rien manger, je suis trop fatigué. *I'm sorry, I couldn't eat a thing, I'm too tired.*

Meeting the Family

Giving your gift

It is a nice gesture to give a present when you arrive to stay with someone. You may like to have a little gift in your hand luggage, ready to offer on your arrival, or you may have it in your suitcase so that you can give it to your host family when you have unpacked. Something typically British, but not too fragile, would be very acceptable.

Here are some sentences that you could say as you hand over your present:

- **Voici un petit cadeau.**   *Here is a little present.*
- **Voici un petit cadeau pour vous remercier.**   *Here is a little thank you present.*
- **Voici un petit cadeau de la part de ma famille.**   *Here is a little present from my family.*

Settling In

Finding your way around the house

You are sure to be shown around the house or flat when you arrive. Apart from names of rooms which you will already recognize, you may soon appreciate that the French, like the English, have some quaint ways of referring to 'the smallest room'. Here are some of them, starting with the obvious:

les toilettes

les W.C. (sounds like "vay say")

les waters (sounds like "vat air")

le petit coin

If you go visiting and need to ask where 'it' is, you should say:

- Où sont les toilettes, s'il vous plaît?
- Où se trouvent les toilettes, s'il vous plaît?

How does it work?

You may find a variety of flushing mechanisms which you haven't come across before; if there is no handle or chain, look for a knob which you might have to pull or press down, or a large button set in the floor which you press with your foot. Tap mechanisms and hand driers in public washrooms work in many different ways – if you are not sure what to do, just watch other people.

French washbasins, baths and bidets often have a different type of plug from the usual English rubber or plastic stopper on the end of a chain. It is usual to find a metal mechanism between the taps which you pull up or push down a few centimetres to raise or lower the plug into position.

Settling In

The question "Comment ça marche?" can be used in any situation when you need to ask how something works. Here are two examples:

Le tampon, comment ça marche? *How does the plug work?*
La douche, comment ça marche? *How does the shower work?*

Your room

Whatever the state of your room at home, you should try to keep your belongings tidy when you are a visitor. If you are not sure where to put things, ask:

Où est-ce que je mets ma valise?
ma trousse de toilette?
mes affaires?
mes vêtements?
ma serviette?

Where do I put my suitcase?
my sponge bag?
my belongings?
my clothes?
my towel?

If you should need an extra pillow, blanket or towel, ask:

- Encore un oreiller/une couverture/une serviette, s'il vous plaît. *Another pillow/blanket/towel, please.*
▶ Je voudrais un oreiller/une couverture/une serviette de plus. *I'd like an extra pillow/blanket/towel.*
■ Est-ce que je peux avoir un oreiller/une couverture/une serviette de plus? *May I have an extra pillow/blanket/towel?*

Settling In

French electrical sockets are two-pin. If you take any electrical equipment with you, buy an international travel plug before you go. If you are not sure which plug to use, ask an adult in the family "La prise, ça va?" ("Is this plug all right?")

Anything you need?

If you should run out of anything essential or forget something important, use the following examples to make the sentences you need.

J'ai oublié/perdu mon savon.	*I've forgotten/lost my soap.*
ma serviette.	*my towel.*
ma brosse à dents.	*my toothbrush.*
mon talc.	*my talc.*
mon déodorant.	*my deodorant.*
ma brosse.	*my hairbrush.*
mon peigne.	*my comb.*
mon shampooing.	*my shampoo.*

Il n'y a plus de papier hygiénique. *There isn't any toilet paper.*

Je n'ai pas de serviette/savon. *I don't have a towel/any soap.*

Je n'ai plus de shampooing. *I haven't any more shampoo.*

Settling In

- Tu me prêtes du savon? *Will you lend me some soap?*
          du dentifrice?   *some toothpaste?*
          du talc?   *some talc?*
          du déodorant?   *some deodorant?*
          du shampooing?   *some shampoo?*

▶ Veux-tu me prêter un peigne?   *Would you lend me a comb?*

■ Est-ce que je peux emprunter une serviette?
                                           une brosse?

   May I borrow a towel?
               a hairbrush?

Bedtime

> As the French often eat late, they do not usually have bedtime drinks, biscuits, etc. If you are offered a drink at night, it is likely to be a 'tisane', a herbal tea which is thought to be soothing and a help to sleep.

When you are ready to go to bed (and, as a visitor, try to be aware of when the family would like to go to bed) you should say:

Je vais me coucher maintenant.   *I'm going to bed now.*

In reply you may hear any of the following:

Bonsoir/Bonne nuit.   *Goodnight.*

Dors bien.   *Sleep well.*

A demain.   *See you tomorrow.*

Fais de beaux rêves.   *Sweet dreams.*

You answer by wishing them in return, "Bonsoir" or "Bonne nuit". The next morning you may be asked:

Tu as bien dormi?   *Did you sleep well?*

Hopefully you will be able to reply:

Oui, très bien merci, et toi (*or* vous)?   *Yes, very well, thank you, and you?*

Fitting In

The French for "Make yourself at home" is "Fais comme chez toi!" However, no thoughtful guest would behave *exactly* as he would at home! As a visitor, you should try not to disrupt the life of your host family unnecessarily. If you follow some of the hints in this chapter, you will feel more at ease with the family and they will appreciate your thoughtfulness.

When is it convenient . . . ?

Enquire about the family routine, so that you do not feel embarrassed or in the way:

- Je me lève à quelle heure?   *What time should I get up?*
- A quelle heure est-ce que je me lève?
- Je dois me lever à quelle heure?

- C'est à quelle heure, le petit déjeuner?   *What time is breakfast?*
- On prend le petit déjeuner à quelle heure?
- A quelle heure est-ce qu'on prend le petit déjeuner?

- Je me lave à quelle heure?   *What time should I wash?*
- La salle de bains est libre maintenant?   *Is the bathroom free now?*
- Ça ne vous dérange pas si je vais dans la salle de bains maintenant?   *Is it convenient for me to use the bathroom now?*

La salle de bains est libre maintenant

Fitting In

If you are going out, you will want to know when to be ready:

- 🟢 **On part à quelle heure?** *What time are we going out?*
- ▶ **On part pour l'école à quelle heure?** *What time do we leave for school?*
- ▶ **On part pour faire les courses à quelle heure?** *What time are we going shopping?*
- ▶ **On part pour faire une promenade à quelle heure?** *What time are we going for a walk?*

It is easy to make up other similar sentences. Notice that the French say "on part . . ." rather than "nous partons . . ."

Asking permission

Je peux prendre un bain/une douche? *May I have a bath/shower?*

Je peux acheter des timbres? *May I buy some stamps?*

Je peux mettre cette lettre à la poste? *May I post this letter?*

J'ai soif, je peux boire quelquechose? *I'm thirsty, may I have something to drink?*

J'ai faim, je peux manger un petit quelquechose? *I'm hungry, may I have a snack?*

Je peux sortir avec mon ami? *May I go out with my friend?*

Je peux téléphoner à mon ami? *May I telephone my friend?*

Je peux téléphoner chez moi? *May I phone home?*

It would be polite to offer to pay for your telephone calls, particularly those to England, even though your offer may be refused.

- 🟢 **Je vous dois combien?** *How much do I owe you?*
- ▶ **C'est combien pour téléphoner en Angleterre?** *How much is it to phone England?*

Washing and Ironing

During your stay you may need to make arrangements to have some of your clothes washed and ironed. This is not usually a problem as the French mother normally offers to do it when she does her family wash. You may hear sentences similar to these:

As-tu du linge sale? Je vais faire la lessive aujourd'hui. *Have you any dirty clothes? I'm going to do the washing today.*

Donne-moi ton linge sale, s'il te plaît. *Give me your dirty washing, please.*

Mets ton linge sale dans la corbeille dans la salle de bains. *Put your dirty washing in the basket in the bathroom.*

Mets ta chemise/tes chaussettes (etc) au sale. *Put your shirt/socks (etc) in the dirty pile.*

However, if nobody mentions the subject you will need to ask:

Où est-ce que je mets mes vêtements sales? *Where shall I put my dirty clothes?*

Est-ce que je peux laver mon linge aujourd'hui? *May I do my washing today?*

Où puis-je laver mon linge?   *Where can I do my washing?*
Où puis-je sécher mon linge?   *Where can I dry my washing?*

Fitting In

The washmark symbols on clothing labels are internationally recognized, so you should not need to explain how to deal with anything delicate. If you have a garment and know that the colour runs, either leave it at home or explain:

Cette couleur déteint au lavage.   *This colour runs in the wash.*

However, if you would rather do your own washing you could say:

Je préfère laver cela moi-même.   *I'd rather wash that myself.*

Chez moi je le fais moi-même.   *I do it myself at home.*

Chez moi je lave toujours mon linge.   *I always do my own washing at home.*

If your clothes are badly creased during the journey, or if you wish to iron something before you go out, you could ask:

Je peux repasser cela, s'il vous plaît?   *May I iron this, please?*

It may happen that you unexpectedly need something washed quickly. You could ask (*very* politely):

Pouvez-vous laver cela pour ce soir/demain, s'il vous plaît?   *Could you wash this for this evening/tomorrow, please?*

Meals

Meals and mealtime customs

If some of the mealtime customs seem strange to you or if you are not sure about how to eat something that you have never tried before, watch how the family behaves and you will soon learn what is acceptable. If all else fails, ask:

Comment est-ce qu'on mange cela? *How should I eat that?*

Meals

Here are some things which you may find unusual:

- at the start of a meal, people may wish each other "Bon appétit!" This means "Enjoy your meal". You reply using the same phrase;
- when not actually eating, French people rest their wrists on the edge of the table (this is not to be confused with *elbows* on the table, which is no more polite in France than it is in England!);
- at the beginning of the meal, you should wait for an adult to begin eating before you start – unless you are told that you may start immediately;
- when you have finished eating, you should leave your knife and fork apart or even with just the tips resting on the plate. There may also be a knife rest beside your plate; you wipe your knife clean on a piece of bread and then rest the blade on this at the end of the course. You will then use this knife for the cheese and fruit courses;

Meals

> - there are still many households where the meat is served as a separate course, followed by the vegetables or salad;
> - French people often use a piece of bread to mop up all the sauce or gravy on their plates. This is not considered bad manners but a compliment to the cook;
> - filling puddings are rarely served; your dessert will probably be ice-cream, yoghurt, fruit and/or cheese.

Accepting and declining food

You are sure to be offered foods which you have never tasted before. Be willing to try everything because you may otherwise miss something delicious, but ask to be served with a small portion if you feel unsure about it.

- Un peu, s'il vous plaît.   *A little, please.*
▶ Un tout petit peu pour essayer, s'il vous plaît.   *Just a little to try, please.*
■ Je n'ai jamais mangé ça; je peux essayer un petit morceau?   *I've never tasted that; may I try a little bit?*

If you like it:

- Oui, j'aime ça.   *Yes, I like it.*
▶ Oui, j'aime ça. Encore un peu, s'il vous plaît.   *Yes, I like that. A little more, please.*
■ Oui, j'aime bien ça. Je peux en avoir encore un peu?   *Yes, I do like that. May I have some more?*

If you don't like it, this is how you refuse politely:

- Non merci, je n'aime pas ça.   *No thanks, I don't like it.*
▶ Non merci, je ne l'aime pas beaucoup.   *No thanks, I don't like it much.*
■ Non merci, je ne l'aime pas tellement.   *No thanks, I don't like it all that much.*

If you *cannot* eat something because you are allergic to it:

Non merci, je ne mange pas ça, j'ai une allergie.

Meals

IMPORTANT!
If you say "merci" when something is offered to you, it means "*No thank you*" in France. If you want to accept, you should say "oui" and/or "s'il vous plaît".

Offering help

At the end of the meal (which will probably last longer than you are used to – the French like to talk while they eat!) it would be polite to offer to help.

- Je peux vous aider?   *May I help you?*
- Je peux enlever le couvert?   *Shall I clear the table?*
- Je peux faire la vaisselle?   *Shall I do the washing up?*
- Je peux essuyer la vaisselle?   *Shall I dry up?*

The art of conversation

This is difficult when you have a limited knowledge of the language, but you can benefit from what you listen to. This may be the one time when the family sits together and talks; you may not follow much of what is said, but try to keep 'tuned in' for some of the time. This may also be the time when you are asked about your day. Here are some questions you may hear with suggested answers:

Qu'est-ce que tu as fait aujourd'hui?   *What did you do today?*
   Je suis allé au collège.   *I went to school.*
   Je suis allé en ville.   *I went to town.*
   Je suis sorti avec mes camarades.   *I went out with my friends.*
   J'ai visité... (somewhere).   *I visited... (somewhere).*

Meals

Tu t'es bien amusé? *Did you enjoy yourself?*
- Oui, très bien, merci. *Yes, very much, thank you.*
- Oui, c'était très bien/formidable. *Yes, it was very good/great.*
- Oui, je me suis très bien amusé. *Yes, I enjoyed it very much.*
- Non, pas beaucoup/pas du tout. *No, not much/not at all.* (but be prepared to explain why!)

Qu'est-ce que tu as vu? *What did you see?*
  J'ai vu . . . *I saw . . .*

If your family asks you questions like these, you could try to prepare a few simple things to say on your way home from wherever you have been, or before the meal. Your willingness to try to speak to them will please them and they will probably help you to get it right. Try to remember that when people correct you, they are not being critical of you but are genuinely trying to help. Don't be afraid of using the same sort of phrase over and over again – at least you will remember those phrases!

Daily Life

Things to talk about

It can sometimes be hard to find general topics of conversation, especially at the beginning of your stay, when you do not know the family very well. Here are some suggestions of things you might take which could start a conversation and help break the ice:

- photos of your family, pets, house;
- an illustrated booklet about your home town;
- a map showing the area where you live;
- leaflets about places of interest near you;
- books about the Royal Family, Britain, London;
- magazines on subjects you are interested in – pop, films etc.

These will give you an opportunity to show your willingness to speak French, even if what you say is rather limited. Everyone knows "Voici..." and "Voilà..." and you could practise some slightly more ambitious sentences before you go.

Daily Life

You might like to take an individual gift for your partner, in addition to the family present. A book can provide a good opening for a conversation. If you know that your partner has a particular interest or hobby (such as music, ballet, railways, aircraft, pets, cars, horses, computers, crafts, pop groups, film stars) an illustrated book in English on that subject would give you both something to discuss.

If you don't know of any particular interest, an English version of a French book, such as one of the Asterix or Tin-Tin series, could provide some fun.

Things to do

Card games, chess, draughts, dominoes – all cross the language barrier, so if you have a pocket set it would be a good idea to take it with you. A pack of cards has the added advantage that you can fill some spare time with a few games of Patience, especially if your partner is occupied with homework and the rest of the family is busy.

Take something with you for those times when you want to be on your own to relax – paperbacks, a personal stereo and cassettes, for example. You won't find television and radio as restful as at home because you will have to concentrate to understand, but you will have fun when well-known series appear with French voices.

Going to school

French children usually wear casual clothes to school but are not scruffy. If you are not sure what to wear, ask your friend:

Qu'est-ce que je dois porter pour aller à l'école?   *What should I wear to school?*

In a similar way, you can ask what to take:

Qu'est-ce que je dois prendre?   *What should I take?*

The answer to that question may include such things as:

un crayon/un stylo/un bic/du papier/un cahier   *a pencil/a pen/a biro/paper/an exercise book*

27

Daily Life

You may be told to be prepared for bad weather:

Prends un manteau. *Take a coat.*
    une veste. *a jacket.*
    un anorak. *an anorak.*
    un imperméable. *a raincoat.*
    un K way. *a cagoule.*

'K way' is a brand name and is pronounced 'Ka-way'. 'Cagoule' in French means a balaclava helmet.

French schools start earlier, sometimes as early as 8.00 am, so it is as well to ask the night before:

On part à quelle heure (pour aller à l'école)? *What time do we leave (for school)?*

If you have to travel on public transport to school, you may be given a 'carte d'étudiant', a student travel card, which you must show.

Arrangements for lessons and for lunch will vary, so make a note of anything you are told.

Daily Life

Going visiting

You may be invited to visit friends or relatives of the French family. These occasions can be quite formal, so it would be as well to ask what kind of clothes you should wear.

Est-ce que je dois porter une tenue habillée? *Should I wear something smart?*

When you arrive, be ready to shake hands and say "Bonjour, Monsieur/Madame".

If there is to be a meal, it will probably last much longer than an equivalent one at home; meals are a very social occasion in France and you should expect to stay at the table for a long time. You may not be able to follow much of the conversation, but if you are included, you may need to ask people to speak more slowly (see the sentences at the beginning of "Don't Worry"). You won't be expected to join in complicated discussions, but be prepared to answer a few questions about yourself, your home and your family.

Sporting activities

There are swimming pools in most towns and there may be a sports complex nearby. When you pack, include a large towel, your swimsuit and sports shoes or trainers. If you have a swimming cap, take it with you, since some pools require you to wear one; in this case there will probably be caps available for hire. You could ask:

On doit porter un bonnet de bain? *Do you have to wear a bathing cap?*

Est-ce que je peux emprunter/louer un bonnet de bain? *May I borrow/hire a swimming cap?*

If you are not the sporty type, don't know how to play a particular game, or just don't feel in the mood, you may find the following sentences helpful.

Je n'aime pas nager.	*I don't like swimming.*
patiner.	*skating.*
Je n'aime pas jouer au football.	*I don't like football.*
au basket.	*basketball.*
au tennis.	*tennis.*
au badminton.	*badminton.*

Daily Life

Je ne sais pas jouer au volley.
                          aux boules.
I don't know how to play volleyball.
                           bowls.

Je n'ai pas envie de nager/jouer . . .   *I don't feel like swimming/playing . . .*

Entertainment

> If you are in a small town, the cinema programme may change several times during the week. Watch out for posters in the café, the tabac and other public places to see if there is anything which might interest you.
>
> The local Casino is not only a place for gambling. It often houses the local theatre where many cultural activities take place, such as concerts (classical and pop), ballet and opera. It may also be the largest available hall where dances and discos can be held.
>
> If you are invited to 'un bal', don't panic, it's not a grand ball, but the name for a dance. In rural areas the dance may be called a 'bal champêtre'; in warmer places, dances may be held out of doors, perhaps on the town or village square.
>
> Panic is also unnecessary if you are invited to a 'boum'. You are not going to get blown up, but are being invited to an informal party.

Out and About

The hints and phrases in this chapter are to help you when you are out with your partner or on your own, whether shopping or sightseeing.

Shops you might need

When you are out shopping, you might want to ask where certain shops are:

- Où est le bureau de poste?
- Où se trouve le tabac?
  - le supermarché?
  - la boulangerie?
  - la pharmacie?
  - la librairie?
  - la pâtisserie?
  - la confiserie?
  - la parfumerie?

Where is the post office?
the newsagent (and tobacconist)?
the supermarket?
the baker's?
the chemist's?
the bookshop?
the cake shop?
the sweet shop?
the chemist's (cosmetics only)?

If you want to ask if you can visit a particular shop:

Est-ce qu'on peut aller au bureau de poste?
au tabac?
à la pharmacie?
à la confiserie?
etc

Out and About

A useful shop – le tabac

You can buy your postcards at the 'tabac' and also post them there. Postage rates are likely to change, so the easiest way to buy the right stamp is to show your postcard to the assistant and say:

Un timbre pour l'Angleterre, s'il vous plaît.

At the tabac they also sell souvenirs, newspapers, magazines and films. It is cheaper to buy your film before you leave home and have it processed on your return. If you want to buy an English newspaper, expect to pay quite a lot more for it.

Opening and closing times

These will vary depending on the area you are staying in. It is not unusual for shops to close for two hours or more in the middle of the day. This also applies to post offices, banks, large stores and tourist offices.

C'est ouvert, le supermarché? *Is the supermarket open?*

Le bureau de poste, ça ferme à quelle heure? *What time does the post office close?*

For other shops, just substitute the name of the shop for those given above. Shops, banks etc will also display their opening and closing times on the door or window.

Out and About

Buying a snack

If you are out with others and your energy is flagging, you might want to ask:

Est-ce qu'on peut boire/manger quelquechose? *Could we have something to drink/eat?*

You could even offer to pay, especially if the family has been very generous to you:

- Est-ce que je peux payer cette fois?   *May I pay this time?*
- C'est à moi de payer.   *It's my turn to pay.*
- C'est moi qui paie.   *This is my treat.*

Your first experiences of ordering food and drink in a bar or café are quite likely to be in the company of your French partner. Watch and listen carefully to what is said and how the business of paying is carried out. You will realise that you do not need to say very much! There will be a menu above the bar to prompt you, so simple phrases will be enough:

un coca	*a coke*
jus d'orange	*orange juice*
café crème	*white coffee*
thé citron, s'il vous plaît.	*lemon tea, please.*

MENU

Jus de Fruit	Sandwichs variés
Café au Lait	Croque Monsieur
Café Noir	Plat du Jour
Thé Simple	Frites
Thé Infusion	Chef Salade
Bière Pression	Crabe Farci
Bière Bouteille	Hamburger Basquaise
Eau Minérale	
Soda	*****
Chocolat	Glaces au Choix

Service non compris (10%)

L'addition, s'il vous plaît.   *The bill please.*

Remember that 'un café' is coffee without milk.

Out and About

> You may either pay the waiter or pay at the cash desk. The
> service charge is nearly always included in the prices on display
> in a café or bar – 'service compris'. If you see the words
> 'service non compris', this means that the service charge is not
> included in the prices shown on the menu. You will still be
> charged for it as an extra of 10% or 12% on your bill! You do
> not have to leave a tip unless the service has been particularly
> good and you wish to show your appreciation.

Buying souvenirs

Whatever you buy, remember that you are going to have to pack it!
Avoid souvenirs which are:

- too big;
- too fragile;
- too heavy;
- illegal.

If you are under 18, you are not allowed to bring cigarettes or
alcohol through customs, not even as gifts for other people. It is not
permitted either to bring fireworks through customs. If in doubt, ask
someone in authority. You would be very unpopular with your group
if customs officers decided to hold you for questioning because you
had brought back something illegal, however innocently.

Buying clothes

Clothes abroad always look tempting because they are 'different'. Clothes in France tend to be expensive compared with English equivalents, so think hard before you decide to buy and check that you will not overspend. There are tables of sizes in the last chapter of the book.

You will find these phrases useful:

C'est combien? *How much is it?*

Je regarde seulement. *I'm just looking.*

Je ne sais pas exactement. *I don't quite know.*

Je peux essayer? *Can I try it on?*

C'est trop grand/petit. *It's too big/small.*

Je n'aime pas la couleur. *I don't like the colour.*

Avez-vous la même chose en bleu? *Have you the same thing in blue?*

Ça me va bien! *It suits me!*

Ça ne me va pas. *It doesn't suit me.*

Ça me plaît! or J'aime ça! *I like that!*

Je n'aime pas ça. *I don't like that.*

Je le prends. *I'll take it.*

Out and About

Keep your money safe

Money can be lost or stolen, so take a few sensible precautions.

DO:
- before leaving home check that you have some secure pockets;
- keep money in an inside pocket or securely closed bag;
- keep money in separate places, eg some in a pocket, some in a purse/wallet;
- think ahead about how much you will need to spend;
- put money away carefully after paying;
- be aware of the possibilities for pickpockets in crowds.

DON'T:
- put your money in the back pocket of trousers;
- carry too much money;
- change too much money at once;
- brag about how much money you have.

Changing money

Before you leave home, buy a small amount of French currency and some traveller's cheques from your bank or building society. You can choose what amounts (denominations) to have the cheques in. It is best to take a mixture of, say, £5 and £10 cheques. This enables you to cash larger amounts at the beginning of your stay and smaller amounts at the end. Do not bring home more foreign currency than necessary because you will have to pay to change it back. You will not be able to change foreign coins back into sterling, so spend them before you come home.

Out and About

You can change your traveller's cheques into local currency in the bank or the 'bureau de change'. You *must* take your passport with you as identification. You may also be asked for a local address, so you might find it easier if you have your French address already written down to show on request.

> In French banks you take your cheque and passport to the desk; do not sign your traveller's cheques until you are at the desk. The amount you will receive is worked out and you are given a piece of paper with all the details on it. You take this paper to a cashier who then gives you the money.

You can say:

Je voudrais changer un chèque de dix livres. *I would like to change a £10 cheque.*

You might hear:

Votre passeport, s'il vous plaît. *Your passport, please.*

Voulez-vous signer, s'il vous plaît. *Sign it, please.*

Votre adresse en France/ici/à (*town name*) *Your address in France/ here/in* (*town name*)

In some banks, especially in cities and large towns, you may find that the entrance to the bank is kept locked. You ring a bell and the door is opened automatically. When you leave, you follow the same procedure.

Sometimes large stores allow you to buy goods using traveller's cheques, but their rates of exchange will not be as good and you could find it difficult to be sure how much you have really paid.

Out and About

Phoning from a call box

Most French public telephones are very modern and easy to use. Take a supply of coins with you. The instructions are illustrated, so take time to look at them and you should have no difficulty. They will also tell you which coins to use.

If your call is not connected or much shorter than you anticipated, do not forget to look to see if you have received any money back.

The tones are different. You can obtain a free demonstration of the tones on a Freefone service in this country before you go.

To phone home from France, you need to dial 1944 followed by your STD code without the first 0, then your home number.

Travelling alone

If you use public transport without your exchange partner, make sure that you know the name of your 'home' bus stop or railway station so that you know where to get off when you come back! Make a mental note of any landmarks which will help you to recognize it.

If you travel on a school bus with your partner you may be given a pass to show the driver.

If you are eligible for a reduced fare, you may need to carry some identification which has your date of birth on it. If this means carrying your passport about with you, you must take extra care to keep it safe.

> On town buses, there may be a system of buying tickets in booklets at a machine or at a 'tabac'. The number of tickets you give up will depend on the length of your journey. If you don't know, ask the driver. Sometimes the tickets have to be cancelled in a machine rather than given up. Once again, watch what other people do.

Out and About

Here are some useful phrases:

Un aller et retour à ... , s'il vous plaît.   *A return to ... , please.*

Un aller simple à ... , s'il vous plaît.   *A single to ... , please.*

Un carnet de billets.   *A book of tickets.*

C'est combien de tickets pour ... ?   *How many tickets is it for ... ?*

La gare, s'il vous plaît. Vous me direz?   *The station, please. Will you tell me when we are there?*

Outings

When you are out with a group or with the family, you will probably go off by yourself for part of the time.

DO: — make a note of *when* and *where* to meet again;
— make sure you understand 24 hour clock times;
— note details of the coach or car you came in; its colour, name, registration number, where it is parked;
— look out for landmarks to help you find your way back;
— use a town plan;
— always carry with you the name and address of the family you are staying with.

Looking after your Health

There are certain simple precautions you can take to look after yourself and to make sure that a minor problem does not turn into a major worry for you and your hosts.

Medicines are, of course, available in other countries. The problem might be in obtaining those you are used to and which you know work for you. This is *not* the time to try out new medicines, skin creams, etc; you might be allergic to them and this will increase your problems.

You should take with you any medicines which you have to take regularly for conditions such as asthma, hay fever, migraines. Take these with you even if you think that it is not the time of year when you usually need them. Conditions like asthma and hay fever may be triggered off by some plant or substance you haven't come across before.

It is also a good idea to take some, or all, of the following, just for emergencies: a few pain-killers; a selection of sticking plasters; indigestion tablets; throat sweets; a small tube of antiseptic cream and an anti-diarrhoea preparation.

Looking after your Health

Some self-help measures

There are plenty of ways to avoid typical holiday illnesses and to deal with simple problems without disturbing your hosts. Here are some examples:

- if you suffer from constipation (often brought on by a change in water or diet) drink plenty and eat as much fresh or dried fruit and vegetables as you can;
- don't eat too much of anything and especially avoid too much fatty food or fizzy drinks before a long car or coach journey;
- try not to get overtired. If you feel you are doing too much and would like a rest, tell your hosts how you feel. They will probably be relieved to have a rest too!

✔   ✘

Looking after your Health

In case of illness or minor accident

Hopefully you will not need this section! If you do, here are the phrases you might need to explain your symptoms and get treatment:

J'ai chaud.   *I'm hot.*
J'ai froid.   *I'm cold.*
J'ai de la fièvre.   *I'm feverish.*
J'ai la grippe.   *I've got 'flu.*
J'ai une toux.   *I've got a cough.*
Je tousse la nuit.   *I cough at nights.*
J'ai mal au coeur.   *I feel sick.*
Je suis enrhumé.   *I've got a cold.*
Je suis malade.   *I'm ill.*

To tell someone about a pain or ache anywhere, use:

J'ai mal au dos.   *My back hurts.*
    au pied.   *My foot hurts.*
    au bras.   *My arm hurts.*
    au ventre.   *I've got stomach-ache.*
    à la gorge.   *I've got a sore throat.*
    à la tête.   *My head aches.*
    à la main.   *My hand hurts.*
    à l'oreille.   *I've got ear-ache.*
    aux dents.   *I've got tooth-ache.*
    aux yeux.   *My eyes hurt.*

In case of minor accident:

Je me suis brûlé la main.
              le doigt.
I've burnt my hand.
           finger.

Je me suis coupé le doigt.
              le pied.
              le genou.
I've cut my finger.
      foot.
      knee.

Looking after your Health

Une abeille
    guêpe
    insecte m'a piqué.
I've been stung by a bee.
    wasp.
    insect.

J'ai un coup de soleil.   *I'm sunburnt.*

To say you need something:

J'ai besoin d'une aspirine.
    d'un comprimé.
    d'un onguent.
    d'un baume à lèvres.
    d'un baume à aphtes.
    des pastilles.
    des sparadraps.
    des serviettes hygiéniques.
    des tampons.
I need an aspirin.
    a tablet.
    some ointment.
    some lip salve.
    some ulcer balm.
    some throat/cough lozenges.
    some sticking plasters.
    some sanitary towels.
    some tampons.

Looking after your Health

If you are likely to suffer from travel sickness, you should warn your hosts:

- Dans la voiture, j'ai mal au coeur. *In the car, I feel sick.*
- Quelquefois, j'ai le mal de la route, mais je peux prendre un médicament. *Sometimes I get car-sick, but I can take a tablet.*

Going to the doctor

If you have to go to the doctor in France, you (or someone with you) will have to pay a bill. Most of this money can be claimed back provided that you obtain an E111 certificate from the DHSS (Department of Health and Social Security) before you leave home. Read the instructions when you receive the E111.

Here are some phrases you may hear the doctor say:

Asseyez-vous. *Sit down.*

Couchez-vous. *Lie down.*

Levez-vous. *Get up.*

Enlevez votre chemise. *Take off your shirt.*

Retroussez la manche. *Roll up your sleeve.*

Habillez-vous. *Get dressed.*

Ça vous fait mal? *Does that hurt?*

Vous dormez bien? *Do you sleep well?*

Vous mangez? *Are you eating?*

Je vous donnerai quelquechose. *I'll give you something for it.*

Revenez me voir. *Come back and see me again.*

Il faut vous reposer. *You must rest.*

If you have to have medicine, make sure that you understand clearly how it is to be taken and how often. Ask the leader of your group to look at the instructions with you, or failing that, ask one of your partner's parents to help you. The French use suppositories much more than we do because the medicine is absorbed into the blood stream more quickly through the walls of the intestine than by waiting for it to pass through the stomach.

Looking after your Health

If you do have the misfortune to be ill, let's hope it will be only a short time before you can say:

- Ça va mieux, merci.   *I'm better, thank you.*
- Ça va très bien maintenant.   *I'm very well now.*

- Je me sens très bien maintenant, merci.   *I feel very well now, thank you.*

Accidental breakages

If you damage or break anything, all you can do is apologise and offer to pay for a replacement:

- Je vous demande pardon, Madame/Monsieur. *I'm very sorry, Madame/Monsieur.*
  Est-ce que je peux vous payer? *Can I repay you?*

▶ Que je suis gauche! Excusez-moi, Madame/Monsieur. *How clumsy I am. Please excuse me.*
  Je peux vous en acheter un autre? *Can I buy you another one?*

Heureusement ce n'était pas le Ming

Mending

If you tear your clothes or lose buttons, you may need help:

J'ai déchiré mon pantalon/jean/pullover. *I've torn my trousers/jeans/pullover.*

J'ai perdu mon bouton. *I've lost my button.*

La fermeture éclair ne marche pas. *The zip is broken.*

Je n'ai pas de fil. *I haven't any thread.*

Je n'ai pas d'aiguille. *I haven't a needle.*

Je ne sais pas coudre! *I can't sew!*

Pourriez-vous me réparer ma chemise/mon pantalon? *Could you repair my shirt/trousers?*

Minor Mishaps

Losing your belongings

Losing belongings can be very distressing, especially if you are in a foreign country. Try to avoid this by taking the following advice:

DO:
- try to pack all you need for any outing into one bag. A rucksack, haversack or bag with shoulder strap will leave your hands free for taking photos;
- put a card with your name and the address of your host family inside your bag, camera case, etc. At least you then have some chance of any belongings you lose being returned to you!
- make a note of your passport number and the numbers on your traveller's cheques and keep that information where you are staying;
- check that you have everything with you when you leave buses, trains, restaurants, etc;
- keep a close eye on your belongings, especially your money, when you are in crowded places.

DON'T:
- carry your passport and cheques around with you unless you are going to change money;
- carry more money than you need for the day.

Minor Mishaps

If you do lose anything, tell an adult as soon as you can:

J'ai perdu mon sac.   *I've lost my bag.*
    mon passeport.   *my passport.*

J'ai oublié ma porte-monnaie.   *I've forgotten my purse.*
    mon parapluie.   *my umbrella.*

J'ai laissé mes lunettes de soleil.   *I've left my sunglasses.*
    mon appareil.   *my camera.*

Getting lost

If you go out alone, carry with you the address of your host family so that you can ask someone the way:

Excusez-moi Monsieur/Madame. Je cherche cette adresse. *Excuse me. I'm looking for this address.*

Je suis perdu. *I'm lost.*

Listen carefully to any directions you are given, remembering:

à gauche	*left*	tout droit	*straight on*
à droite	*right*		

Observe the same caution about speaking to strangers and accepting lifts as you would when at home. Ask a policeman for help if possible.

Minor Mishaps

Saying no

If someone invites you to do anything you don't want to do or go anywhere you don't want to go, you can be polite but firm in the way you say no.

- Non, merci. Je ne veux pas. *No thanks. I don't want to.*
- Je n'aime pas ça. *I don't like it.*
- Ça ne me plaît pas. *I don't like that.*
- Ça ne m'intéresse pas. *I'm not interested.*
- Non, merci. Je ne fume pas. *No, thanks. I don't smoke.*
- Non, merci. Je ne bois pas la bière. *No, thanks. I don't drink beer.*
- Je ne veux pas l'essayer. *I don't want to try it.*
- Ça ne me dit rien. *It doesn't appeal to me at all.*

Homesickness

This is a perfectly natural feeling, especially if this is your first time away from home, and it is nothing to be ashamed of. For most people it passes very quickly once the strangeness of new surroundings passes and they settle in. However, there are some factors, like tiredness or boredom, which aggravate the feeling.

If you are feeling exhausted by the effort of being with strangers in a strange place, listening to and trying to speak a strange language, give yourself a break and an early night.

- Je suis très fatigué. Je voudrais me coucher. *I am very tired. I would like to go to bed.*

Or ask if you could sleep late the next morning:

- Est-ce que je peux faire la grasse matinée? *Could I have a lie in?*

Minor Mishaps

Try not to be alone with nothing to do. Write a letter or postcard home telling them about all the good things that have happened. If you find yourself pouring out your misery on paper, carry on writing if it makes you feel better – but don't post the letter! Your family wouldn't receive it for days, by which time you will be feeling much better. Take a good book with you, one which you will find relaxing. Think hard before you phone home; will it cheer you up or make you feel worse? If you sound miserable, will they be worried about you at home?

Wish you were here...

Your partner may not be used to having to entertain visitors. You may have to take the initiative and suggest something to do: a game, a film, a walk or a visit to a family where one of your friends is staying.

Est-ce que tu veux jouer aux cartes?
jouer aux échecs?
jouer au football?
voir un film?
aller en ville?
visiter mon ami?
faire une promenade?

Would you like to play cards?
play chess?
play football?
see a film?
go into town?
visit my friend?
go for a walk?

Minor Mishaps

If your partner is busy with homework or something else which you can't join in, you may be able to do something with another member of the family. You could even offer to help with the chores!

Est-ce que je peux vous aider?   *Can I help you?*
Est-ce que je peux vous aider   *Can I help you*
   dans la cuisine?   *in the kitchen?*
   dans le jardin?   *in the garden?*

If you should be unable to hide your feelings, you can tell your partner:

J'ai la nostalgie.   *I feel homesick.*

Ma famille me manque.   *I miss my family.*

It is very likely that by the time you reach the end of your stay you will not want to go home! Many people enjoy their visits so much that they return again and again and find lifelong friends.

What if you don't fit in?

Exchange visits are not always easy but it is rare for them to be a complete disaster. In spite of all the efforts made by organisers, people don't always get on. Asking two young people who have never met to spend quite a long time together and to get on well is asking a lot! They have the added disadvantage of difficulty in talking to one another! The secret must be that people don't expect too much from this new friendship too quickly and that they try to be patient and understand the difficulties.

If you think things are not going as well as you had hoped, look through this checklist and see if you can do anything to improve the situation.

DO:
- remember that the exchange wouldn't be happening if your partner and family had not requested it. They want it to be a success too;
- try to be adaptable to the family's routine and 'house rules', even if they are very different from your own;
- be prepared to try new foods;
- be brave and start to speak some simple French straight away. Let the family realise that you are 'practising' on them and ask them for their help in correcting you. In this way, everyone remembers that they have a common aim;

Minor Mishaps

- consider that your partner may be shy and you may sometimes have to suggest things to do;
- be aware that *your* shyness may come across as unfriendliness or moodiness. Try a smile!
- make a quiet exit if your partner decides to throw a tantrum or have a row with parents, brothers or sisters, provided that you can do this without it being too obvious. You don't want to be put in the position of having to 'take sides';
- try to make some time when you can be alone and when you leave the family alone. If circumstances permit, you could go to your room to write postcards, look at a magazine or listen to your own music. Half an hour alone will be restful for you and may give the family a chance to talk about personal matters;
- consider that you may have more in common with a brother or sister of your partner than you have with the partner;
- remember that the stay is not a long one. Think positively and make the most of the good things;
- talk to your organiser *early* about any problems which you feel unable to cope with. They should have the tact and the language to be able to sort them out before they get out of hand.

DON'T: — expect to be entertained non-stop. You are going to experience family life — and who expects that to be exciting all the time!

Finally

DO: — remember that when your partner comes to share your home, school and friends with you, he or she will have all the same anxieties and difficulties as you have. Try to make the experience a happy and useful one.

The End of your stay

Preparing for the trip home

Pack in good time in case you need to repack because you have bought so many souvenirs!

Remember to leave out whatever clean clothes you are going to need for the day you travel home. Check that you do not leave behind your night clothes, slippers or anything in the bathroom. Pack any gifts as near the top of your suitcase as is safe because a customs officer may want to see what you have bought.

Pack your passport safely but somewhere easy to get at because you will have to show it at the passport control. Make a list of any gifts you have bought and their price; you can show this if you are stopped when you go through customs. Even in the Green (Nothing to Declare) channel, spot checks are sometimes carried out.

There are customs restrictions not only for adults but also for young people. There are different regulations depending on whether you are under 15, or in the 15–17 age group. If you are travelling in a party, your leader will have a copy of the regulations; if you travel independently, you should receive a copy with your ticket. The rules are also displayed at ports and airports.

Do not agree to bring back anything, parcels, packets, bags or bottles which someone asks you to bring back as a favour. You could be getting involved in something illegal. Obviously this need not apply to any presents you bring back from your host family to your own family.

The End of your stay

If you suffer from travel sickness, or if the weather is stormy or very windy, take a tablet against travel sickness about 30 minutes before you are due to depart. As the tablets may make you thirsty, take plenty to drink or make sure you have enough money to buy drinks during the journey. Use up any French coins you have left on the journey, because banks will not change coins back into English money. If you want to buy food, avoid anything rich or fatty, especially if the crossing is rough.

Thanking your host family

To the parents you could say any of the following:

- **Merci beaucoup pour un très bon séjour.** *Thank you for a lovely stay.*
- **Merci beaucoup, Monsieur et Madame. J'ai été très heureux chez vous.** *Thank you very much. I have been very happy here.*
- **Je vous remercie pour toute votre gentilesse.** *Thank you for all your kindness.*

To your partner you could say:

- **Merci mille fois.** *Thanks a lot.*
- **Merci bien. Tu as été très gentil.** *Thanks very much. You have been really kind.*
- **Merci beaucoup. J'ai passé un séjour formidable.** *Thanks very much. I've had a super time.*

When the French family say their farewells you may hear:

Viens nous revoir. *Come and see us again.*

Viens passer encore un séjour chez nous. *Come and spend another holiday with us.*

The End of your stay

Écris nous souvent. *Write to us often.*

Bon voyage! *Have a good journey!*

If there were any particular meals or dishes which you really enjoyed you may like to ask the French mother for the recipes before you leave.

J'aime bien... Vous pourrez me donner la recette, s'il vous plaît? *I enjoyed... Could you give me the recipe, please?*

Writing a thank you letter

Soon after you return to England you will probably want to write a letter thanking your host family. Here are some sentences to help you compose a polite letter to the parents:

Chers Monsieur et Madame... *Dear Mr and Mrs...*

Je vous remercie pour un heureux séjour. *Thank you for a happy holiday.*

J'espère que toute la famille se porte bien. *I hope that all the family are well.*

J'attends avec plaisir la visite de... *I'm looking forward to... visiting.*

J'attends l'arrivée de... avec beaucoup d'impatience. *I'm really looking forward to... coming.*

Quand... viendra chez nous, j'espère que nous pourrons lui offrir la même hospitalité que vous m'avez montrée. *When... comes to us, I hope we can make him/her as welcome as you made me.*

The End of your stay

Merci encore une fois de tout ce que vous avez fait pour moi. *Thank you again for all you did for me.*

J'espère qu'on se reverra bientôt. *I hope we'll meet again soon.*

Avec mes remerciements et mes sentiments les plus respectueux. *With many thanks, Yours sincerely*

Writing to your partner

When you write to your partner after your stay, you could use some of the following:

Mon cher.../Ma chère *Dear (to boy)/Dear (to girl)*

Merci beaucoup pour un séjour formidable. *Thanks for a terrific time.*

Je me suis très bien amusé(e). *I enjoyed myself a lot.*

J'attends ton arrivée avec plaisir. *I'm looking forward to your arrival.*

Écris-moi bientôt. *Write soon.*

J'aime avoir de tes nouvelles. *I look forward to hearing your news.*

Veuille offrir mes meilleurs souhaits à ta famille. *Please give my best wishes to your family.*

A bientôt. *See (or hear from) you soon.*

Amitiés *Love from*

Appendix

Checklist of essentials to pack

Passport
French money and traveller's cheques
E111 Certificate
Enough spare underwear
Nightwear, slippers or soft shoes
Dressing gown or bathrobe if not too bulky
Casual (not scruffy!) clothes
One 'smart' outfit
One pair of waterproof shoes
Waterproof coat, anorak or cagoule
A warm sweater
Handkerchiefs or tissues
Small first-aid kit
For girls, sanitary towels or tampons, even if you think you don't need them
Small amount of writing paper and envelopes
A pen
Gifts for your exchange family
Addresses of friends or relatives you want to send postcards to
Home phone number or number of friend or neighbour
The name, address and telephone number of your exchange family
Phone number and address in France of your trip organiser
A book to read
Playing cards, solitaire or other small game
This book!

Leave at home

Your address and telephone number in France and the family's name
Name, address and telephone number of your trip organiser

Appendix

Useful Comments and Exclamations

Ways of expressing pleasure and approval:

C'est bon! *It's good, nice!*
C'est beau! *It's lovely!*
Chouette! *Great!*
Très bien! *Very good!*
J'aime bien ça! *I like that!*
Pas mal! *Not bad!*
Avec plaisir. *With pleasure.*
D'accord. *O.K., I agree.*
Tu as raison. *You're right.*

Formidable! *Fantastic!*
Magnifique! *Marvellous!*
Naturellement. *Naturally, of course.*
Pourquoi pas? *Why not?*
Bonne idée! *Good idea!*
C'est possible. *That's possible.*
Ça y est! *That's it!*
Ça m'est égal! *I don't mind!*
Bon alors! *Right then!*

Ways of expressing negative ideas, displeasure or disapproval:

Non, je ne veux pas. *No, I don't want to.*
Ça ne va pas. *It's not O.K.*
Ça non! *Definitely not!*
Je n'aime pas ça! *I don't like that!*
C'est impossible! *That's impossible!*
Jamais! *Never!*
Rien! *Nothing!*
Ça m'énerve! *That gets on my nerves!*
C'est ennuyeux! *It's boring!*
J'en ai assez! *I've had enough!*
J'en ai marre! *I'm fed up with that!*
C'est affreux! *It's awful!*
C'est agaçant! *It's annoying!*
C'est dégoûtant! *It's disgusting!*

Other comments:

Un moment. *Just a minute.*
J'arrive! *I'm coming now!*
J'arrive dans un instant. *I'll be there in a minute.*

Appendix

Je reviens dans un instant.   *I'll be back in a minute.*
Eh bien . . .   *Well . . .*
Bientôt.   *Soon.*
Plus tard.   *Later.*
Je n'arrive pas à . . .   *I can't manage to . . .*

Some useful questions:

Ça va?   *Is that O.K.?*   Comme ça?   *Like this? Like that?*
Comment?   *Pardon?* (When you don't hear)
Je peux?   *May I?*   Vraiment?   *Really?*
C'est vrai?   *Is that true? Is that so?*
Est-ce qu'il faut prendre . . . ?   *Should I take . . . ?*
Par ici ou par là?   *This way or that?*
Pourquoi?   *Why?*   Quel jour?   *Which day?*
Quand?   *When?*   A quelle heure?   *What time?*
A quoi sert cela?   *What's that used for?*

Good wishes:

Bonne chance!   *Good luck!*   Bon anniversaire!   *Happy birthday!*
Bon appétit!   *Enjoy your meal!*   Joyeux Noël!   *Happy Christmas!*
Bonne nuit!   *Goodnight!*   Bonne Année!   *Happy New Year!*
Bon voyage!   *Safe journey!*   Joyeuses Pâques!   *Happy Easter!*
Bonne journée!   *Have a good day!*

Saying thank you:

Merci.   *Thank you.*
Merci beaucoup.   *Thank you very much.*
Merci mille fois.   *Thank you so much.*

Saying sorry, etc:

Pardon.   *Sorry.*   Je m'excuse.   *I'm sorry.*
Excusez-moi.   *I'm sorry, please excuse me.*
De rien.   *Don't mention it.*   Pas du tout.   *Not at all.*
Ça va.   *It's all right.*

Appendix

Get the day and date right:

lundi	*Monday*	vendredi	*Friday*
mardi	*Tuesday*	samedi	*Saturday*
mercredi	*Wednesday*	dimanche	*Sunday*
jeudi	*Thursday*		

le premier mars   *1st March*   le vingt et un juin   *21st June*
le deux avril   *2nd April*   le vingt-cinq juillet   *25th July*
le trois mai   *3rd May*

Get the time right:

Official timetables will use the 24 hour clock, so:

douze heures   *12.00 noon*   dix-sept heures   *5.00 pm*
treize heures   *1.00 pm*   vingt et une heures   *9.00 pm*

As in English, there is more than one way of saying certain times

Neuf heures et quart   *9.15*   Dix heures trente   *10.30*
Neuf heures quinze   *9.15*   Dix heures quarante-cinq   *10.45*
Dix heures et demie   *10.30*   Onze heures moins le quart   *10.45*

And if you can't understand:

Je ne comprends pas.   *I don't understand.*
Voulez-vous répéter, s'il vous plaît?   *Will you repeat that please?*
Plus lentement.   *Slower.*
C'est dans le dictionnaire?   *Is it in the dictionary?*
Qu'est-ce que ça veut dire?   *What does that mean?*
Comment ça s'appelle en français?   *What is that called in French?*

Appendix

Sizes

Shoe and garment sizes differ from the ones we use in England. Use the tables below to help you choose the nearest equivalent size.

Shoes

British	2	3	4	5	6	7	8	9	10	11
French	35	36	37	38	39	41	42	43	44	45

Shirt collar sizes

British	14	$14\frac{1}{2}$	15	$15\frac{1}{2}$	16	$16\frac{1}{2}$	17
French	36	37	38	39	40	41	42

Dresses

British	8	10	12	14	16	18
French	34	36	38	40	42	44

Sweaters

British	32"	34"	36"	38"	40"	42"	44"
French	80cm	86cm	91cm	97cm	102cm	107cm	112cm

Height

Feet/inches	5'	5'2"	5'4"	5'6"	5'8"	5'10"	6'
Centimetres	152	157	163	168	173	178	182

General

grand	*large*	court	*short*
petit	*small*	long	*long*
moyen (moyenne)	*medium*		

For your information

If you want more information about the area you will be visiting, you could write to:

> The French Government Tourist Office
> 178 Piccadilly
> London W1V 0AL

You could ask for the address of the local 'Office de Tourisme' for the area where you will be staying.

Appendix

Games to play on the road

To reach your partner's home you may have to travel a long way and you might like to make up some games with your friends to relieve the monotony of motorway travelling. Here are some ideas:

Spot the Département

You can spot where cars come from in France by looking at the last two numbers on the number plate.

01	Ain	34	Hérault
02	Aisne	35	Ille-et-Vilaine
03	Allier	36	Indre
04	Alpes-de-Haute-Provence	37	Indre-et-Loire
05	Hautes Alpes	38	Isère
06	Alpes Maritimes	39	Jura
07	Ardèche	40	Landes
08	Ardennes	41	Loir-et-Cher
09	Ariège	42	Loire
10	Aube	43	Haute-Loire
11	Aude	44	Loire-Atlantique
12	Aveyron	45	Loiret
13	Bouches-du-Rhône	46	Lot
14	Calvados	47	Lot-et-Garonne
15	Cantal	48	Lozère
16	Charente	49	Maine-et-Loire
17	Charente-Maritime	50	Manche
18	Cher	51	Marne
19	Corrèze	52	Haute-Marne
2A	Corse-de-Sud (Corsica)	53	Mayenne
2B	Haute-Corse	54	Meurthe-et-Moselle
21	Côte-d'Or	55	Meuse
22	Côtes-du-Nord	56	Morbihan
23	Creuse	57	Moselle
24	Dordogne	58	Nièvre
25	Doubs	59	Nord
26	Drôme	60	Oise
27	Eure	61	Orne
28	Eure-et-Loir	62	Pas-de-Calais
29	Finistère	63	Puy-de-Dôme
30	Gard	64	Pyrénées-Atlantiques
31	Haute-Garonne	65	Hautes-Pyrénées
32	Gers	66	Pyrénées-Orientales
33	Gironde	67	Bas-Rhin

Appendix

68	Haut-Rhin	82	Tarn-et-Garonne
69	Rhône	83	Var
70	Haute-Saône	84	Vaucluse
71	Saône-et-Loire	85	Vendée
72	Sarthe	86	Vienne
73	Savoie	87	Haute-Vienne
74	Haute-Savoie	88	Vosges
75	Paris	89	Yonne
76	Seine-Maritime	90	Territoire-de-Belfort
77	Seine-et-Marne	91	Essonne
78	Yvelines	92	Hauts-de-Seine
79	Deux-Sèvres	93	Seine-St-Denis
80	Somme	94	Val-de-Marne
81	Tarn	95	Val-d'Oise

By looking at these numbers and the map, you can plot your journey across the various 'départements' and can tell how close you are to your destination.

Appendix

European Vehicle Stickers (showing country of origin)

A	Austria	I	Italy
AL	Albania	IRL	Ireland
AND	Andorra	L	Luxembourg
B	Belgium	MC	Monaco
BG	Bulgaria	N	Norway
CH	Switzerland	NL	Netherlands
CS	Czechoslovakia	P	Portugal
D	West Germany	PL	Poland
DDR	East Germany	R	Romania
DK	Denmark	RSM	San Marino
E	Spain	S	Sweden
F	France	SCV	Vatican City
FL	Liechtenstein	SF	Finland
GB	Great Britain	SU	Soviet Union
GR	Greece	YU	Yugoslavia
H	Hungary		

a) Who can see the most different country stickers?

b) Write down all the letters seen on vehicles in one minute (or in five minutes or longer if you're not on a motorway) then choose three additional letters of the alphabet and see how many words it's possible to make. The game could be played using the letters to make English words and then afterwards to make French words.